At Last We Enter Paradise

AT LAST
WE ENTER
PARADISE

Richard Jones

COPPER CANYON PRESS

Acknowledgments

American Poetry Review: "The Shadow," "The Lullaby," "My Father's Buddha," "The Loft"; *Bluff City*: "Athens Airport," "The Twelve-Year-Old Drunk," "The Oriental Carpet," "The Lake"; " *The Contemporary Review*: "Drinking with My Mother and Father," "The Abandoned Garden," "Thanksgiving"; *Dial-a-Poem Chicago!*: "The Fence Painter," "Certain People"; *Graham House Review*: "The Color of Grief"; *Green Mountains Review*: "Faith"; *Hubbub*: "The Helicopter Pilot"; *Manoa*: "Wild Guesses"; *New American Poets of the 90s*: "Certain People"; *Onthebus*: "The Wedding Party," "Prayer," "Girl with Skateboard," "Black-Out," "The Gift," "The Examination," "The Impossible," "The Fence Painter," "The Mother's Song," "Andrew"; *Pequod*: "Back Then," "White Towels"; *Poetry*: "My Painting," "Things," "Song of the Old Man," "Certain People"; *Poetry Chronicle* (India): "White Towels," "My Painting," "A Vision"; *The Quarterly*: "Today I Saw My Child," "The Visit," "The Poet's Heart," "Letter of Recommendation from My Father to My Future Wife"; *Quarry West*: "Desire"; *Silverfish Review*: "The Abandoned House," "The Dead Calf"; *Zone 3*: "Boundaries."

Some of the poems in *At Last We Enter Paradise* originally appeared in two limited editions, *Walk On* (Alderman Press, 1985) and *Sonnets* (Adastra Press, 1990).

Publication of this book was made possible in part by a grant from the National Endowment for the Arts. Additional support was provided by the Lannan Foundation.

Copper Canyon Press is in residence with Centrum at Fort Worden State Park.

Library of Congress Cataloging-in-Publication Data
Jones, Richard, 1953-
At last we enter paradise : poems / by Richard Jones.
p. cm.
ISBN 978-1-55659-042-9
I. Title.
PS3560.052475A94 1991
811'.54--dc20 91-72063

COPPER CANYON PRESS
P.O. Box 271, Port Townsend, Washington 98368

Contents

THE SHADOW / 9

Part One

THE ABANDONED HOUSE / 13

THE DEAD CALF / 14

GRIEF, 1942 / 15

TWELVE-YEAR-OLD DRUNK / 16

GIRL WITH SKATEBOARD / 17

DESIRE / 18

THE WEDDING PARTY / 19

THE LULLABY / 20

THE LOFT / 21

THE VISIT / 22

THE AMPUTEE / 23

THE EXAMINATION / 24

AFTER MAKING LOVE, I TELL A GHOST STORY / 25

BLACK-OUT / 26

FAITH / 27

THINGS / 28

THE LAKE / 29

TODAY I SAW MY CHILD / 30

WHITE TOWELS / 31

THE IMPOSSIBLE / 32

PRAYER / 33

THE HELICOPTER PILOT / 34

THE MOTHER'S SONG / 35

THE GIFT / 37

THE COLOR OF GRIEF / 38

ANDREW / 40

THE ORIENTAL CARPET / 41

Part Two

BACK THEN / 45

CRAZINESS / 49

WILD GUESSES / 52

ATHENS AIRPORT / 54

CERTAIN PEOPLE / 55

DRINKING WITH MY MOTHER AND FATHER / 56

LETTER OF RECOMMENDATION
FROM MY FATHER TO MY FUTURE WIFE / 57

MY PAINTING / 59

MY FATHER'S BUDDHA / 61

THE POET'S HEART / 63

THE FENCE PAINTER / 64

THE ABANDONED GARDEN / 65

THANKSGIVING / 66

SONG OF THE OLD MAN / 67

A VISION / 68

BOUNDARIES / 70

FOR THOSE
I DIDN'T LOVE ENOUGH

The Shadow

Tonight we give up the idea
of night, and now,

darkness,
what shall we do with you?

With light,
who is extinguished?

Everyone, everyone.

All but the shadow, the voice
thrown down in the dirt to burn.

PART

ONE

The Abandoned House

Glass cracks underfoot,
dust lifts into light,
flowered wallpaper
blooms and fades,
and everywhere the sad
sweet smell of urine.
The broken stairs,
a test of faith,
ascend to a window
composing the world—
dirt road, valley,
village in the distance,
and, on a far hill,
a small, white,
freshly painted,
empty wooden church.

The Dead Calf

Snow has fallen,
and a mournful lowing
drifts through a slate-gray mist,

bringing the farmer
puttering into clarity
with his son on a slow blue tractor.

The machine idles
as the boy jumps down
and strikes the cow with a stick,

whipping her
to the edge of the field,
where she calls across the pasture

as her heavy calf is carted away
in the baling arms of the tractor.

Grief, 1942

AFTER THE PHOTOGRAPH BY DMITRI BALTERMANTS

In Crimea at the end of winter,
an old woman trudges through mud,
searching among the dead
for her son
while soldiers stand guard.

In her long black coat,
she approaches a corpse,
cries out,
bends down,
opens her arms,
but does not find,
here among so many others,
her son in this body,

this body she gave birth to
and named.

Twelve-Year-Old Drunk

Singing, he staggers
down my street, a half-
empty pint in hand.
Whiskey whirls him
as if he were dancing
in crazy wild circles
and falling down laughing
to wait for the world
to stop spinning.
But he's not laughing,
and the world keeps spinning.
He lies on my lawn like a little old man,
everything suddenly sad.
Even the stars look sick to him.

Girl with Skateboard

She dries herself with a frayed white towel
before the window in her hospital room,
tempting the world with her boyish body,
though the world will never have her.

Down in the park, tiny people
remind her of germs.
Her mother can't come until evening.
Today, everything's making her blue—

friends who say *each day is special*,
the get-well flowers and the slowly dying
heart-shaped helium balloons,
even her purple skateboard, propped in the corner like a gun.

She ties a kerchief
on her head like a pirate
and climbs into bed with her teen magazines,
pictures of boys she'd like to kiss.

Her hand caresses the bud of her breast;
two fingers slip between her legs where she's wet.
She closes her eyes to dream of men
who could have loved her in life,

where all she's known is the rush of skating
in traffic up one-way streets,
drivers honking and cursing
as she passed them in the wrong direction.

Desire

Knowing our desire for details,
the evening news tells us
how the man died, and even a little
of how he lived, his work, and whom he loved.

He worked in an office downtown.
At night he rode the train home.
There's the point of entry: the broken window.
There, the bed where he was sleeping

when he heard the intruder. Now
the camera hurries through the house,
like a reader skimming pages,
to the room where his life

is outlined in chalk
and the knife is held up to the lights.

The Wedding Party

In the clear April sky
over the wedding party
gathered on the beach,
the drunken best man
was flying his Cessna.

He was doing tricks—
loops and rolls—
buzzing the beach
above the beautiful
barefoot bride and groom.

But a single-engine Cessna
is a small plane, its power
limited.
When the best man aimed it skyward
into the curve of a high chandelle,
at the top of the arc
the engine stalled—

and the best man fell to earth
and the newlyweds ran toward the fire.

The Lullaby

When she had the abortion
she didn't tell me.

She took a taxi to the clinic,
signed her name,

and waited with the other women
and one young girl who was sobbing.

That night she told me
she was tired.

She went to bed early
and turned on the fan—

its music helped her sleep—
and through its blades she heard me

singing
as I washed and put away the dishes.

The Loft

I lay on her bed
while she opened windows
so we could see the river
and the factories beyond.
Afternoon light falling
beautifully into the room,
she burned candles,
incense, talking quietly
as I listened—
I, who conspired
to make this happen,
weaving a web of words that held
this moment at its center.
What could I say now?
That I am a man
empty of desire?
She stood beside the bed,
looking down at me
as if she were dreaming,
as if I were a dream,
as if she too had come
to the final shore of longing.
I lay, calm as a lake
reflecting the nothingness
of late summer sky.
Then she spoke—
she said my name—
and I, who did not love her,
opened my arms.

The Visit

My ex-wife blushed and unbuttoned her blouse,
revealing her breasts, the puckered nipples,
and, what I most wanted to see and taste,
the miraculous thin white stream of milk
sputtering and shooting into the air.
Her white shirt open and loose like curtains,
she lifted her baby, offering her breast,
blind nipple in the V of her fingers;
and the child, quiet now, sucking, drinking,
held onto her breast with his greedy hands
until he fell asleep there, sinking deep
into the pure clear dark of infant sleep.
Then I held the baby and tried not to think,
while she buttoned her shirt and fixed us drinks.

The Amputee

My brother-in-law is a doctor.
He cuts off people's legs.
Yesterday at dinner,
between the chicken and the lemon pie,
the phone rang. I heard him
tell the resident,
"You *have* to cut if off."
The resident was young;
he didn't want to do it.
Like my brother-in-law,
I'm older, more experienced.
I've been cutting off
parts of myself for years now
to save my life.

The Examination

"After work, I begin with gin,"
I tell my new doctor,
"three martinis, very dry,
straight up, with olives,
which I drink while preparing dinner.
I live alone,
but set a table—
white cloth, two candles, music,
a bottle of dry red wine
to accompany the meal.
Then I read or watch tv,
sipping beer until I'm sleepy,
sleepy enough to shuffle off
to bed with a snifter of cognac."

While the doctor takes notes,
I think
of Poe. *He drinks,*
wrote Baudelaire,
with speed and dispatch,
as if trying to kill
something inside him,
some worm that will not die . . . .

The doctor says
"Stop."

The fool wouldn't let me leave
until I swore an oath,
lifting my hand as though making a toast—

to the souls of my unborn children.

After Making Love, I Tell a Ghost Story

Years ago
in this room
where we sleep,
a boy was shot
in a quarrel
over money.
His mother
closed her eyes
and fell over the body,
crying *Lord, Lord,*
as if God might take the bullet back.

Sometimes at night
you can hear her grief,
the grief that haunts this room.
Listen: what we hear
when we make love
is the old woman crying.
She is the terrible muse
who sings us to sleep each night,
the one who watched grief's seed,
the bullet,
blossom in this room,
peopled now

only with darkness,
and tears,
and death,
and us.

Black-Out

Our last night together,
a summer storm struck
and the house went dark.
When the sky cleared
and the stars came back,
we sat on the high balcony,
drinking wine, talking in German
about Berlin and Barcelona,
remembering our tiny bed in Paris
and the sleepless nights.

When it was time to say good-bye,
we grew quiet.
Inside the dark house
you lit a candle
and asked me in English
to follow,
the woman I loved
lighting my way
and unlocking the door to the dark.

Faith

How can I tell you all the things
I regret? How can I tell you
I never loved enough? How can I
speak of shame, never having spoken
of it before? And in what voice
should I speak, and how should I approach you—
with my shoulders back, as though I am proud
of who I am, proud that I am
now human enough to confess? If I am

to speak to you, it must be
in a low voice—you will have to lean forward
to hear me; my breath will touch you,
lightly, on your cheek. And your breath, too,
will touch me, like the thinking of a god
who never speaks, but is listening.

Things

I go to a dimly lit second-hand store
to lift empty champagne glasses
and open dusty drawers.
I buy the broken chair
and dedicate myself
to its new life.
I leave with the chipped vase,
the cracked violin, the yellowed lace.

I go to bright department stores
where aisles of merchandise
sing their songs
beneath fluorescent lights—
desks, sofas, picture frames
asking for a reason to exist,
demanding our secrets, our love,
every thing demanding
everything of my life.

The Lake

Each day like a water jug—
filled, emptied, refilled.
I take off my clothes
and walk across the meadow.
So much that is impossible to resolve.
The path is uneven,
my body sways like a woman's.
When I reach the lake,
green and deep and cold,
I stand by the water for a long time
before diving in.

Today I Saw My Child

Today I saw my child
floating down over the lake,
shimmering in the light,
coming down to rest on the water.
Turning her face to me,
I saw she was the burst seed
of a dandelion,
the soft stuff of a weed.
She floated on the water,
the green water;
my daughter floated on the water.
I thought I heard her singing,
though it may have been
the light, or the breeze,
or the silent sound the water makes
when it translates for the child,
saying, "Look, father, I am everywhere.
You can touch me.
I am not lost."

White Towels

I have been studying the difference
between solitude and loneliness,
telling the story of my life
to the clean white towels taken warm from the dryer.
I carry them through the house
as though they were my children
asleep in my arms.

The Impossible

FOR MY NEPHEW, 1978–1984

We could be together now,
years later,
sitting on my tattered sofa,
you with your root beer,
me with my bourbon,
watching tv as I explain
the beautiful art of baseball.
Bottom of the eleventh:
the Cubs came back
with three in the ninth to tie
and now the impossible
happens—a rookie,
just up from the minors,
pinch hits and wins the game.
I am trying to tell
the significance of this.
You snuggle under my arm
and listen,
looking first at me,
then at the television.
But you are still young
and don't understand
though you know enough of love
to look at me
and tell me that you do.

Prayer

When I go to bed
I think how far away I am
from the people I love.
I live in a farmhouse
in the middle of a field
bounded by woods
at the foot of the mountains
in Virginia. From my window
I watch cows slowly cross the pasture.
My wife lives in Boston.
My father and mother live by the sea.
My sister lives by a river.
She stands in the kitchen
and looks out and sees
her living son climbing the tree,
her dead son walking on water.

The Helicopter Pilot

His face is ghoulish
in the green and blue lights
of the cockpit's gauges.
Hovering, he shines

a light on the river,
then slowly descends;
the water backs away
in ever-widening circles.

When people gather
by the water's edge
around a boy's body
laid on a blanket,

his job is done.
He turns his light off
and the sound—
like a scythe—

fades into the night.

The Mother's Song

AFTER GEORG TRAKL

It was evening.
We were playing together under a tree.
You were curled inside
an old tire tied by a heavy rope
to a high branch.
I was swinging you,
catching you now and then
to cover your face with kisses,
each kiss like a wish
dropping into a deep blue well.
Mother and child. It was enough
just to look at one another
in the cool autumn dusk
as a purple sweetness
settled down from the stars.

I left you only for a moment.
You walked down the stone steps
toward the river,
a blue smile on your face,
and in the calm of your few small years
you died.

That night I stood in the garden
as moonlight poured over flowers and leaves
a silver, inconsolable grief.
I wanted to call your name
but you were a bouquet
in my heart being torn to pieces.

And now, at the hour
when the sun is purple
and a white heron wades in the water,
you appear,
quietly.

Taking my hand,
you lead me under the elms
by the river.
We drop blue petals into the water
while the shadows darken and widen and become one.

The Gift

Because we see the grave
is the size of a door

we would go with him.
But the ground is open

only to one
and love thrown down

in the earth is lost
forever. Now

loving each other
is all we have left.

But who among us
is strong enough

to carry the terrible
gift he has given?

The Color of Grief

We drop petals
on the water
in his memory,

as if he
and the river
were one.

We talk
about him
while the flowers float away.

How lucky we are
he died
in the river behind our house,

where the ducks he loved
waddle up the lawn.
How much better

to remember him here,
where the river whispers
he's alive!

than at the grave,
where his five years
are carved in stone,

and the hardened earth
is silent,
and grief is green

and always edged
with dying flowers;
for we know grief

is blue, like the river,
which takes our flowers
when they are fresh

and carries them away.

Andrew

This is the way I remember my nephew:
at the children's museum in Boston,
sculpting something strange from clay
he said was his mother and Rusty his dog,
connecting electrical wires
to switch on red revolving lights,
climbing the small fireman's ladder
through hanging sheets of red cellophane
to the window of the tiny house,
like a hero.

At the hotel pool
I taught him to dive.
I called him Superman
when he bravely bellyflopped,
then held his body on top of the water
while he kicked across the shallow end.
Thomas, his brother, jumped off the board
making a goofy face.
Kate looked up from her book and laughed,
the way she'd laugh later
when she showered with Andrew
and he kissed her on the fanny.
And I remember, when we got home
he picked flowers for his mother—
snapped the blooms off
the neighbor's prize roses,
threw away the thorny stems,
and offered her only blossoms
in his cupped, dirty hands.

The Oriental Carpet

Nights like this when I can't sleep
my dog stays with me,
curled on the worn oriental carpet
I bought at a yard sale
the day the truck hit the lost dog,
a dog that could have been her sister,
they looked that much alike.

It was evening. Summer.
The truck kept going.
I dimmed the lights,
stepped from my car
and knelt down in the road
next to the dog.
She lay still,
blood oozing
from her mouth and anus.
Someone brought a blanket.
The dog looked up at me.
A man stood over us,
shaking his head.
A woman came out of her house,
backed up her station wagon
and opened the rear door.
We lifted the dog
onto the blanket,
into the car.
Then I drove away,
the red carpet slumped
like a body in the backseat.
Half-way home I noticed

my emergency lights
still flashing—
two green arrows
on the dashboard,
pointing in opposite directions,
beating furiously.

Now my dog's sitting before me,
staring into my eyes.
She'll walk in a circle on the carpet
and then come back.
When it's this late
all she wants for us
is sleep,
to lie down like dogs
on the oriental carpet,
close our eyes,
let go of our bodies
and die a little,
yes, die a little.

PART

TWO

Back Then

Back then I was broke,
so I painted houses
in the neighborhood
during the day
and worked nights
downtown in a warehouse,
lifting crates of beans
and sacks of rice till dawn.
I preferred painting houses,
working high on a ladder,
alone in the light, my face
speckled with paint,
to the dreary graveyard shift,
the dirt and concrete,
the dim fluorescent lights
and endless droning of forklifts.
But I made good money
those nights in the warehouse
hauling crates to the docks,
loading the trucks and learning
the difficult camaraderie of men;
or learning to fight,
if that's what they wanted,
as two of us fought one night,
driving our forklifts into one another.
He was the quick-tempered foreman
who once held his knife to my throat.
He had the long fingers of a concert pianist
and the strength of any five of us,
but owned no home
and slept in back of the dark warehouse

between walls of cardboard boxes.
I wanted to kill the son-of-a-bitch.
And he wanted to kill me,
but after we fought
he shook my hand
and stole melons from the freezer,
which we ate as the trucks pulled out
and the clean light came
to wash away the night.

Back then I'd come home
at dawn and drink beer,
telling my father about the nightshift
while he shaved and dressed for work,
and after he was gone I'd sleep a little
on the damp and twisted sheets,
white curtains bright at the window
in the attic of my parents' house.
I remember those mornings—
going down to the kitchen
where my mother ironed and cooked.
She worked with great seriousness
in the everyday world of the house,
stopping for coffee and a cigarette
to stare out the window
a few minutes in silence.
I never asked
what she was thinking,
but her loneliness
made me think of my father,

a salesman for Dominion Tobacco.
I wondered if she imagined him
as I still did—the young pilot
flying secret missions
over the bamboo jungles of China,
his mask with the rubber air hose
dangling from his face like an elephant's trunk.
As a boy I feared my father flew
with a cargo of bullets and bombs.
But when I was older I learned
my father flew supplies—
crates of food like the ones I loaded
on trucks each night at the warehouse.

As my mother went back to work,
I'd finish my coffee and bread,
kiss her good-bye,
and enter the cool summer morning.
I'd climb to the highest eaves
of the house that took all summer to paint.
I'd drift through the hours,
clearing away cobwebs
or burning wasps' nests,
washing away pigeon shit
or scraping peeling paint
until the wood was smooth.
Then I painted the old house red
with one ten-dollar horsehair brush
and twenty-five buckets of paint.

There was never any money
for me in painting houses.
To make a living you've got to work fast.
Along the edges where white met red,
I'd hang on the ladder for hours
trying to make the lines run true.
But when the house looked good,
people admired the work.
And sometimes I'd look down and see
my father bringing something to eat.
He'd call to me, forty feet up,
Be careful!
then stand and watch me working.
My father understood
the danger of painting tall houses—
his brother fell
and broke his neck.
But I never fell.
I'd finish working
where I was on the ladder,
paint my brush dry
and climb down to join him.
We'd sit in the grass
and eat our sandwiches,
gardens blooming
like paradise around us—
my father and me
talking about work
and what we would do
someday with our lives.

Craziness

The faces of people I've never seen,
a black dog,
a bleak blue hill with bare trees
that could be mistaken for unpeopled crosses—
these are the subjects of my paintings.
My style is primitive;
my method, physical.
I stand on the canvas and fling paint from two brushes,
swirling my arms in crazy wild circles
and leaping back and forth all night
above a canvas that resembles childhood's empty sky.
I love my paintings
but throw them away,
still wet in the morning.
Now that it's dark, I'll paint my body blue
and sleep on the canvas.
When I wake I'll nail the piece to the wall
and call it *Richard,*
Dreaming.
Perhaps by now you have guessed
I am not in love
and live alone.
But don't mistake me for a painter:
I'm a professor of English.
In a drawer I keep my early, unfinished poems.
They could have been written by anyone
but me.
Perhaps I should complete
that bastard-of-a-last chapter
of my dissertation,

Poetry and Becoming
in the Early Unknown Work
of Another American Poet.
The title is impressive,
but my theme of the spirit coming to life
and looking for its voice
is difficult
and resists me.
Perhaps I should surrender
to a more mystical process, the way
spirit loves words into being, the way
I would love you
if you broke down the basement door
to find me sleeping
with brushes and knives
and unfinished manuscripts.
All I ask
is that you be
a compassionate critic
and bring me a cup of coffee.
Listen to me,
you Rationalists, you Naturalists, you Neo-classicists.
Écoutez:
Répétez la phrase:
Je suis Victor Hugo
passed out on the basement floor.
Now that you've awakened me
be kind:
help me up.
Walk with me.

Mornings like this, I like to go out
and walk down the alley
with the garbagemen.
It is healthy to know the physical weight
of things we throw away,
goods touched by who-knows-how-many hands,
and now touched by your hands,
by the gloved hands of the garbagemen,
and by my hands,
naked
and unprofessional.
That's why I listen
for the truck rumbling up the alley
and open the back gate and help the men
throw trash into the big truck's belly.
A garbage truck, like a poet,
welcomes everything—
broken windows, chicken bones, old poems,
uneaten pills, empty metal buckets, a child's glove,
even these painted pictures of imagined people,
this portrait of a black dog,
this bleak hillside with bare blue trees
one might mistake for crosses.

Wild Guesses

I retreated from the world
to the cottage on the cliff,
wanting to live
like a hermit again,
to lose myself in the fog.
Those gray days of mist and rain
I was happy, content
until the wind cleared the fog
and the snow-capped mountain
across the bay
appeared like the god
of another country.

It was, I think, a Tuesday morning.
I stood at the kitchen window
doing dishes. All week
at that window, I'd witnessed
miracles—deer nibbling
the bushes, the blossoming flower
whose name no one knew,
the swift rolling rivers of mist.
Another morning, another oracle
telling me about my life.
Mist signified the thinking
that confused me. The deer stood
for tenderness. The blossoming
was everything beyond the six letters
of beauty. Was I wrong to want
the mountain to mean
something grand and symbolic?
The Indians named the mountain

Koma Kulshan, Great White Watcher,
and went on with their lives.
Now there are no Indians
to teach the language
of understanding.
So I turned away from the window

and turned on my typewriter
and read Keats, now
a decade younger than I.
I read Rimbaud, even younger.
I slipped Mozart, the prodigy,
into the boombox
and went outside.
It was drizzling.
I pulled dry logs
from the damp woodpile
and carried them in to the stove.
I took my morning's sip of bourbon
and ate a piece of bread.
The dishwater bubbled and popped;
grease floated on the surface;
the sonata filled the room.
I put a match to the gas
under the pot of cold coffee
and wrote you a letter
composed of wild guesses
on the meaning of mountains
while the fire blazed
and the house puffed out messages
a hundred years old.

Athens Airport

I never made it to Athens—
a bombscare in Madrid
grounded the plane
and everyone was evacuated.
I waited in a bar with two Swedes
who insisted on buying me drinks
while soldiers searched our suitcases
with dogs and machines.
When the loudspeaker told us
in seven different languages
the plane was secure
and would soon take off,
the still-sober Swedes
ordered another round,
but I was already bombed
on fear and *cerveza*.
I leaned against the bar's tinted windows
and watched my plane lift off,
its three white lights disappearing
into the night with the Swedes
and my rucksack on board.
But I still had my moneybelt and passport.
I still hadn't seen the Alhambra
or the Costa del Sol. I hadn't been to Africa.
The next day I bought a second-class train ticket south
and three bottles of wine.
I shared a compartment with four teenage girls
who giggled when I lifted a bottle and said "*Por favor?*"
But I was happy riding with these dark-haired angels
and felt no desire to tell them about my wandering life,
where I was going, or how all my things were lost
and spinning in circles in the airport in Athens.

Certain People

My father lives by the ocean
and drinks his morning coffee
in the full sun on his deck,
speaking to anyone
who walks by on the beach.
Afternoons he works
part-time at the golf course,
sailing the fairways like a sea captain
in a white golf cart.
My father must talk
to a hundred people a day,
yet we haven't spoken in weeks.
As I grow older, we hardly talk at all.
I wonder,
if I were a tourist on the beach
or a golfer lost in the woods
meeting him for the first time,
how his hand would feel in mine
as we introduced ourselves,
what we'd say to each other,
if we'd speak or if we'd *talk*,
and if, as sometimes happens
with certain people, I'd feel,
when I looked him in the eye,
I'd known him all my life.

Drinking with My Mother and Father

My mother and father arrive
for their annual visit.
They tell me they love me.
They open a bottle of wine.
Salute. Health.
We spend the day together
under trees, drinking.
My mother gets a little tipsy
and tells a dirty joke.
My father swirls his glass
and tells a long, involved,
convoluted story
that makes no sense at all.
Just like them,
I, too, get a little high
and tell stories all day.
"How wonderful!" we say,
"How wonderful!"

As the sun sets
we stagger off
to a bed of pine needles
on the hill beside my house.
Stones under our heads
softer than pillows,
we watch the sky grow dark.
How quiet we become,
and a little sad,
when the evening sings
and the stars come back,
but even our sadness
has a flavor like wine.

Letter of Recommendation from My Father
to My Future Wife

During the war, I was in China.
Every night we blew the world to hell.
The sky was purple and yellow
like his favorite shirt.

I was in India once
on the Ganges in a tourist boat.
There were soldiers,
some women with parasols.
A dead body floated by
going in the opposite direction.
My son likes this story
and requests it each year at Thanksgiving.

When he was twelve,
there was an accident.
He almost went blind.
For three weeks he lay in the hospital,
his eyes bandaged.
He did not like visitors,
but if they came
he'd silently hold their hand as they talked.

Small attentions
are all he requires.
Tell him you never saw anyone
so adept
at parallel parking.

Still, your life will not be easy.
Just look in the drawer where he keeps his socks.

Nothing matches. And what's the turtle's shell
doing there, or the map of the moon,
or the surgeon's plastic model of a take-apart-heart?

You must understand—
he doesn't see the world clearly.
Once he screamed, "The woods are on fire!"
when it was only a blue cloud of insects
lifting from the trees.

But he's a good boy.
He likes to kiss
and be kissed.
I remember mornings
he would wake me, stroking my whiskers
and kissing my hand.

He'll tell you—and it's true—
he prefers the green of your eyes
to all the green life
of heaven or earth.

My Painting

In my painting I am flying
in a 1927 Sopwith Camel bi-plane,
the kind flown in the early war,
with Jesus as my pilot.
We are flying reconnaissance
over a field of wheat
where red cows meditate on the blue
mountains in the distance.
In the bottom right corner of the painting,
a circle of children dressed in white
are dancing, celebrating
the eternal life
to come. In the bottom left,
in a purple house, my mother and father
are lying on long wooden tables,
peacefully, surrounded by the glory
of pink geraniums blooming
in heavy clay pots.
When Jesus and I fly past,
the flowered curtains flutter
and the children look up.
Jesus waves good-bye, then
points the plane heavenward,
his eyes raised toward the stars
above the painting. I look
back at the half-finished earth,
at the children and the cows and the house.
There are some last touches I'd like to make,
a little more color, a lake perhaps
with silvery fish leaping
over nets in the water like rainbows.

But Jesus, his eyes on heaven,
doesn't look back, and the plane
is climbing, faster and faster,
and I realize now
he won't turn back
even if I
tried to explain
that I'm not finished with my painting
and my painting is not finished with me.

My Father's Buddha

When I was a boy
and afraid of the dark,
I'd steal downstairs
when everyone was sleeping
and kneel before the old sideboard,
my father's liquor cabinet.
I was learning to drink,
each night turning a key
and opening two small doors
as if this were the beginning
of a long dark book.

One night I discovered something
hidden behind the bottles—
a small wooden statue of the Buddha,
lacquered gold,
inlaid with precious stones,
colored glass and bits of mirror—
a statue my father stole
during the war from a village
in Burma. The Buddha
was the only thing he took
when the troops looted the temple.

I was thirty-three,
my father's age during the war,
and had finally stopped drinking
when he told me this story
one winter morning over tea.
He unlocked the cabinet
and gave me the statue,
wrapped now, carefully,

in clean white muslin.
He never asked to be forgiven;
he simply lifted it into the light.

Now the Buddha sits on my desk,
compassionless, half-smiling,
mindful as I devote myself
to the task within the gift,
to do as my father taught me:
save one thing
and offer it to the morning sun
which sees all things
for what they are.

The Poet's Heart

Think of the Buddhist monks
who sat in the road
at the start of the war,
saffron robes soaked in gasoline,
and set themselves on fire.

Think of the violence,
the immolation, the composed desire
for peace
silently spoken to ashes;
think of the gift,
the eloquence of their burning.

Poems, too, burn
like a body on fire,
devoted, implacable,
not in flashing epiphany,
but steadily, like the priests
and the world they could imagine.

Think, too, of Shelley's drowned body
burning on the beach in Italy,
of Trelawny, who reached
into the fire
to steal the poet's heart.
The poet's heart:
what the fire could not consume.

The Fence Painter

By the time I wake,
the fence painter is ready
to knock off for the day.
The black lines of the fence
fall away behind him
more evenly, more beautiful
for the touch of his brush.
His forearms black with asphalt paint,
as though part of the brush and bucket,
he concentrates on the unfinished wood
until it matches to his satisfaction,
an unblemished darkness he imagines.
"I like to start early," he says,
"before the sun gets too hot."
I can't say whether he's happy,
but I envy the fence painter
the early morning hours
and the peace of hard work,
the way he puts away his tools in the afternoon
and drives home in his truck.

The Abandoned Garden

In late October it rains.
The house grows chill and dank.
Out back, the abandoned garden,
gone to seed beneath the frost,
desolate under a half-moon.

Not yet November,
but already cold enough
to light the stove.
That's good—

long nights before the fire,
reading and drinking tea—

as good as summer days,
my shirt on a nail,
my hands in the dirt.

Thanksgiving

Today I cleaned the gutter's garbage
and raked the lawn's litter of leaves,
then lugged the stuffed green plastic bags
out back behind the garage.

I pulled dead stalks of flowers
and snipped the perennials. I turned the soil
until the dirt fell black and loose
from my shovel, then scraped the beds smooth.

Tired of summer's confusion of growth,
I appreciate winter's order,
the season composed of less and less
until nothing's left
but the outline of the garden's border.

Song of the Old Man

I might have died when I was young,
my body all muscle and desire,
and believed death was beautiful

but then I would have missed
the beauty of the body's
decline, how we fall

away like a flower,
surviving the season
to bloom just once,

throwing sweet scent into the air
and becoming a part of everything there.

A Vision

Last night I found myself
alone on a beach at sunset,
my back to a vast, glittering city.
I was the only witness
to the mountain rising
out of the sea toward heaven.
I thought it was the land of the dead,
but saw no people, not even a tree,
only rock and sand, sickly green
in the waning daylight.
I ran through the streets
back to the high-rise apartment,
took the elevator to the top,
to tell my father, my mother,
join me—hurry—
by morning the vision may be gone—
but my parents had been dead for years.
My sister came in from the study,
an open book in her hands,
and calmly asked me,
"Hasn't Andrew taught you anything?"
And then I realized how beautiful it is
to talk with the dead
who appear as mountains
in visions that send you running
back to the living.
I opened the sliding glass door
and stood on the balcony
beneath the empty evening sky
and looked without grief

at the city's million lights
sparkling like heaven,
illuminating the city where people I love
and people I've never met
wait for the quiet moment
when at last we enter paradise.

Boundaries

AFTER MA CHIH-YUAN

If the crow
perched on the dead branch
of the apple tree,
his back to the dark,
sees the sun setting
behind the ridge of pines,
the broken fence where a skinny horse
searches for grass,
the spring brook flowing
between the road and my house,
then he also sees me
opening my door and crossing
the rickety little bridge
that connects me to the world.

Richard Jones was born in London and educated at the University of Virginia. His first book of poetry, *Country of Air* (Copper Canyon Press, 1986), won the Posner Award from the Council for Wisconsin Writers. He is also the author of four limited editions of poetry, *Windows and Walls* (Adastra Press, 1982), *Innocent Things* (Adastra Press, 1985), *Walk On* (Alderman Press, 1986), and *Sonnets* (Adastra Press, 1990). Since 1979, he has edited the distinguished journal *Poetry East* for which he received a CCLM Editor's Award in 1985 and a CCLM Special Commendation in 1988. He is also the editor of two critical anthologies: *Poetry and Politics* (Morrow, 1984) and *Of Solitude and Silence: Writings on Robert Bly* (Beacon, 1982). He is a professor at DePaul University in Chicago.

CPSIA information can be obtained
at www.ICGtesting.com
Printed in the USA
LVOW08s1515130518
576633LV00011BA/2/P